JANET SHEPPERSON

The Aphrodite Stone

SALMON POETRY

Published in 1995 by
Salmon Publishing Ltd,
Upper Fairhill, Galway

© Janet Shepperson 1995

The moral right of the author has been asserted

The Publishers gratefully acknowledge the support of
The Northern Ireland Arts Council

A catalogue record for this book is available from the British Library

ISBN 1 897648 03 0

Cover illustration by Sue Smickler
Cover design by Poolbeg Group Services Ltd
Set by Poolbeg Group Services Ltd in Palatino 10/15.5
Printed by Colour Books, Baldoyle Industrial Estate, Dublin 13

The Aphrodite Stone

To Nick, with love
and gratitude for his unfailing support

Acknowledgements

Ireland: Madonna of the Spaces (Lapwing), *Cyphers, Poetry Ireland Review, The Salmon, Fortnight, Windows, Belfast Telegraph, Gown Literary Supplement/The Big Spoon, Honest Ulsterman Ulster Newsletter, Living Landscapes Anthology*.
'Rosguill' was read on 'All Arts and Parts,' Radio Ulster.

The Tyrone Guthrie Centre at Annaghmakerrig

UK: *Poetry Review, Stand, The Rialto, Poetry Wales*.
'A Great Brown Bog of a Coat' won a prize in the Bridport Arts Centre Creative Writing Competition.

US: *Southern Review, Seneca Review*

Canada: Map-Makers' Colours (Nu-age Press, Montreal)

Contents

Dancing on Ice (1963)

Come in, girls. Playtime's over. Kennedy's been shot.
The world is holding its breath. We're watching history
being made on a tiny black-and-white screen we've wheeled
into the gym (where it's warm). Now, girls, come in.

> We're out here on the ice,
> polishing up our slides,
> our breath is steam in the air,
> our feet are slipping sideways,
> circling to a new song
> for slides: *Let's twist again,*
> *Like we did last summer …*

Come in, girls. Summer's over. The newspapers have pictures
of Lee Harvey Oswald – they say he was a Marxist –
they say the fear of communists in America could grow
into a red nightmare, raise tensions in Berlin
and many other cities – in this divided world –

> In this divided world
> boys sit one side of the hall,
> girls sit the other, and wait
> to be asked up. Not us.
> We don't need boys to help us
> wriggle and slither and scream
> and swoop across the ice –

Come in, girls. Ice is dangerous. And a woman is still a
woman.
Every girl should have a career for a while – until she
marries.
Even that space woman, Valentina Tereshkova,
has married an astronaut: the world's first space couple.

Who's going to wash the dishes
when they get home from space?

Well, she is, I suppose. But that's hardly the point.
A woman needs a man, she needs a shoulder to lean on.
Think of the fun your mothers had in the Forties:
nightingales
singing in Berkeley Square, his arm round her waist,
protectively. Her white-gloved hand flirting in his …

We need our hands free
for balance, learning the steps
of a dance that has no steps.
Our heads don't know what's happening
but we're thinking with our feet …

Do you want to be left out, facing middle age
with no partner at all? For the last time, girls, come in.

No more wallflowers,
no one two three, one

two three, in the gym, waiting
to be swept off our feet by *him*.
For the first time dancing apart,
heartscared and proud,
out here, on our own
two feet. We won't come in.

The Belfast Urban Area Plan (Revised)

I dreamed I saw the City Hall subsiding –
wavering like a drunk, its straight lines buckling,
its grey hide wrinkling, all its legs giving way,
till it sank down with a sigh like a cow in a meadow

full of daisies. The air was heavy with humming,
loud as a thousand bees. I passed the Lord Mayors,
stiff on their pedestals, straight-faced under pigeon shit,
respectable as only dead men can be,

and Frederick Temple, Marquess of Dufferin and Ava,
Canadian Governor General, Viceroy of India,
his chest a tangle of tassels and medals that must be
stunting his growth, the way ivy strangles a tree trunk.

When I rounded the corner, the ground was littered with
fragments
like twigs, or prunings, smooth and grey and bulbous,
and the humming was louder. Women in yellow helmets
were ignoring the trees, and having a go at the statues:

their chain saw took a chunk out of a frock coat,
buttons bounced on the grass, a stern beard juddered
and went sailing through the air. *Stand clear*, they told me,
this lot are all coming down. There exists a shortfall

4

of recreational space in the Inner City.
Look at that fellow – you couldn't say he was exactly
recreational. Besides, he's rotten
inside, you hear him creaking when it's stormy

– if he comes down on your head, you'll know all about it.
We plan to plant small trees here, flexible
enough to bend with the wind, they won't strike poses
or preach or rant – the perfect Urban Forest.

The last I saw was Carson up at Stormont;
his hand, that had pawed the air for decades, quivered
as the hum of triumphant bees rose to a crescendo,
and he dropped his fingers and clutched his plinth as they came.

Private Viewing

She's a small person loitering nervously
in the corner of a warehouse full of paintings.
They're paintings of the gaps between things.
She crouches in the gaps and hates the paintings
because they're all about the way each time
she opens her mouth it comes out wrong and people
listen but their arms are folded against her,
their bodies are saying *Is that the time? I must go.*

She's a single woman menaced by the cosy
grumpiness of marriages, by the dazzle
of radical feminists in huge shiny earrings
and by herself in the mirror at seven a.m.
saying *Your hair is all wrong and there's a muscle*
at the corner of your mouth that won't stop twitching
and you embarrassed me yesterday, creeping about
avoiding people's eyes at the private viewing.

Up a dusty staircase in the warehouse
is the part they ignored when they made it into a gallery:
a small room full of scaffolding left by the builders
and torn out plumbing and rusty pipes and railings.
It reminds her of the heap of old scrap metal
squatting on the dockside, where the wind
whistles through the gaps and sometimes kids
climb precariously up the twisted rungs.

She thinks she'd like to take it to work with her,
and tether it to her desk – mentally adding
some buckled pram wheels, claws from a JCB,
the guts and entrails of a burnt-out bus,
the skeleton of a scooter she had as a child.
But where it would be most at home is in
the warehouse, downstairs at the viewing, labelled
Installation With Gaps And Small Person,

surrounded by people sipping wine, assessing
the work's importance and each other's reactions,
and she'd be a pair of eyes in the midst of the heap,
peering out at the drinkers through the gaps.

A Great Brown Bog of a Coat
I.M. Tony O'Regan 1945-1991

I'm sitting in this conference of men,
flexing my feminist muscles, ready to strike
in with the right abstraction; *infrastructure*,
prestigious, potential – their words

grind past like juggernauts – *development*,
disposal. But there's nothing here my tired,
uncertain mind can jump up and get hold of –
just a sense of movement – speed – no brakes.

She slips into an empty chair. She fidgets
beside me in a tangle of soft green
that looks near-edible. *I love your jumper*,
I whisper to her. *Yes*, she says, *it's moss-stitch*.

It makes me think of hillsides, barren rock
and ravaged screes, the way they gather fragments
of green around themselves, criss-crossing, deepening,
spreading to cushioned lushness, taking in

water and light, producing scraps of rainbows.
And that's a gorgeous coat you have, she says.
A great brown bog of a coat. The guilty pleasure
of colours, textures, curves – almost subversive –

laps round our conversation, as we sink in
acres of tweed, dark flaky chocolate colour
of turf, flecked with bog-cotton, heather stems
twisted to ancient shapes, steeped in the bubbling

cries of curlews. All across our mountains
traffic has gouged deep ruts; a photo taken
at night shows darkness punctured by red lines
of tail-lights, sharp as barbed wire. Picture us

huddling in the spaces, oozing out
between the lines, like grass or earth or water
seeping towards the motorways, under cover
of winter, gnawing their edges, gathering strength.

Clichés

They straighten out your seething,
random, multi-coloured,
confusing undergrowth,
and comb away the tangles,
plaiting it into fat buds
that swell out into bluebells
 – each mauve curve artfully
poised, to give the impression
of playfulness controlled.
They smile and smile and smile,
choking all other growth.

You try to root them out –
squashy things that won't
survive the summer, flattening
themselves against the earth,
abject, drained of juice,
yellow, dog-eared, dead.
One good storm will snap
their paper stems, leave only
a few bleached rattling seedheads,
easy to gather and burn.

You rake the soil, leave winter
to break up the surface nicely.
You fail to notice the tiny
bulbs that have burrowed like maggots
under your skin, and are fattening
in the darkness, multiplying
and stretching, ready to nudge
your thoughts aside with their green
glossy complacent snouts.

Iconostasis

Crammed with icons, sagging under
the weight of saints and heroes frozen
in the act of dragon-spearing, or
brandishing books or unexplained arrows.
Eagles peer down. Pelicans.
Byzantine shades to baroque: a Virgin
with clouds and cherubs, sheeted in plastic,
kissed by the faithful. Gilded by love
and money, wreathed in pineapple leaves,
fish scales and feathers up to the ceiling.

I feel them pushing me back. They're meant to.
Only the priests – all men – may enter
the sanctuary. A velvet curtain
fills the doorway, keeps at bay
the horned gods, the goddesses –
Athena, Artemis, Aphrodite.
I twitch the curtain aside: a clock
(modern), dusters, cleaning fluid.
From a hook on the whitewashed wall
the priest's black robes hang like bats' wings.

Church of the Archangel Michael

Among the olive trees, the small dome broods
like an outdoor oven: walls the colour of bread:
no windows. Doors thrown open once a year
on Michael's feast day: no electric lights,
no gold iconostasis topped with dragons,
with lamps that swing on chains from gilded snouts,

just close, earthy darkness.
A woman dressed in black
lighting matches, pointing;
figures on the walls.
'This – Mary and Jesus.
This – John the Baptist.
This – Saint Helena.
This – Saint Lazarus.'
Hands uplifted, haloes,
wings, solemn eyes
staring down until
she runs out of matches,
out of English words.

Eight centuries of damp and candle smoke
have tarnished the bright robes, nibbled the feet,
cobwebbed the heads that bend to us, benign
or ominous, then fade, retreat to where
they've always been: the dark behind our eyes.

Watching the Parade at Larnaca

Along the Palm Tree Promenade, four deep,
they line the route and wave heart-shaped balloons
as the procession moves sedately past
Theo's Bar, the Dolphin Restaurant.
Silver trumpets glitter, scarlet banners
sway with tassels, lanterns, filigree,
meek sailors in white hats and solemn girls
in white gloves guide a huge beribboned cross,
decked out with flowers, under lines of flags:
Greece is blue and white, Cyprus is gold –
an undivided island – with green leaves.

No matter that it hasn't rained for months
and nothing is green and UN soldiers pace
up and down barbed wire in Nicosia
and the woman with what seems to be a gold
chain of office, beaming, keeping step
with the Patriarch in his lush embroidered robes
may turn out to be only the President's wife.

No matter. In this handful of photographs
taken from a hotel balcony
it's always the moment after a day of rain
when every face in the crowd is turned towards

her smile – relaxed and easy – genuine.
No-one has eyes for the Patriarch; the sun
has just come out in time to show her shadow,
regal, an inch or two ahead of his.

Aphrodite

The sun peels scent from eucalyptus trees.
Behind a locked gate, archaeologists
have staked their territory, burrowing
patiently through a warren of Gothic arches
and under that, the tawny crouching curves
of an older church, Byzantine, huddled in earth,
and under that, the oldest Christian symbols:
bread, wine, a fish, a cross, Roman mosaics
among the broken columns of Greek marble.
And under that, it stops. No trace is left
of Aphrodite with her shining hair,
her worshippers bringing grain and oil and grapes,
carved stones, clay figurines. Destroyed perhaps
by an earthquake tossing and fracturing this ground
that was sacred long before the Romans came.

Our footsteps tap along the wooden walkway
into the church that now stands islanded
above the excavations. Still in use.
A jumble of icons, bits of embroidery,
spluttering candles, heaters, microphones.
We look for Aphrodite in the smile
of the reticent Virgin, stiffly cradling her child,
but her hair is tucked away in a silver halo
and even her hand, raised awkwardly in blessing,
is silver, or silver-plated, set in a mould.

Perhaps Aphrodite is in the white doves preening
themselves in a fan of daylight at the door.
Perhaps she is outside basking in the sun
on a patch of neglected ground, where anemones
spread petals like shreds of cloud, filled with dark stamens
the colour of dried-up blood, lying back watching
us with shining, hurt, impatient eyes.

Ballynafeigh, Winter

Snow thickens like scar tissue,
blunting the red white and blue
accusations of kerbstones,
smoothing the scratches left
on pavements by the hot
shattered glass of July.

Across the Lagan, docile
rows of redbrick animals
crouch at the river's edge,
frost flattening their ears,
white fur on their muzzles,

staring with half-closed eyes
into the wind's cold brightness
that sifts its silence over
the grey tide's hesitation.

Ballynafeigh Honey

It could be something harmless, of course.
A noise in the attic's not that strange
in a house this age, I tell myself.
If you're lying awake, put it down to stress.

Yes. But it could be water clumped
in a sagging pool just over my head.
That click, click could be drip, drip,
till the last drop makes the plaster crack
and down it comes in a cold dank flood.
Or, in the sick half-light before dawn,
when it starts again, that drip, drip
could be tick, tick. Something that doesn't
care whose attic it pulls apart,
whose windows it shatters, whose bed is crushed
under rubble, splinters of glass, dust.

I decide to make a phone call.
A man comes with a ladder.
Into the loft, then out,
whistling. 'What you have
is a bees' nest. Or a wasps'.
I can't see: it's too dark.
'There's some wee hole somewhere
they're getting in by – just

the size of your fingertip.
Not much point trying to shift them –
they'll always find a way back.'
I stand on the ladder, press
my ear against the eaves:
the murmuring of bees
in immemorial attics.

Forget about wasps. Think honeycomb.
Shining hexagons, clammy with sweetness.
Send your thoughts ranging up and down
from Cherryvale Field's massed daffodils
to the windy curve of the Lagan. Ignore
the human geography – which streets
are mixed, and which are marked out by
Protestant colours, *No Taigs Here* –
just follow the flightlines, nuzzling into
foxgloves, fuschia, lavender
from the weeded borders of Rosetta
to the shaggy grass of the Ormeau Park,
lifting gold from horse chestnut candles,
searching the hearts of snapdragons,
bringing back to the attic a glut
of information you'll give in your dense
intricate clicking circling dance,
letting other bees know the provenance
of the glittering pollen of Ballynafeigh.

And when, in autumn, the dance slows down,
try not to think about workers, drones
foundering, starving. Maybe they die
outside. Buried under leaves. Devoured
by hedgehogs. Crows. Anything's better
than tiny wizened corpses clogging
the hive. It needs to be left clean
for the hibernating one – the queen
curled up oblivious till spring
wakes and sends her blundering
fatly, furrily into each cell,
laying new eggs. Or so I tell
myself – insisting the bees must go on
filling the crumbling, empty loft
with their dance and their honey long after I'm gone.

Fog

It hatches from tiny eggs
all over the city, embedded
in bushes, in wild flowers trailing
from the gutters of derelict roofs;
every cluster of green has spawned
an amoeba that yawns and stretches,
beginning to take control,
cutting off the ends of streets,
pushing away the sky
where helicopters scratch
and whine like insects, trapped.

Its flow interferes with distances.
It completely moves Cavehill
from an afternoon in October
to somewhere in your mind,
where only essentials remain –
dew on blackberry leaves,
red earth between the pines,
black earth under the heather.

The fog tide rises. Its waves
break at your feet, with fragments
of driftwood and filtered light

and all you need to survive
on an isolated shore,
two hundred and fifty metres
above the dissolving city.

The Scapegoat at Carlingford Louth

I stand on the pebbled shore at Rostrevor,
my back to the placid Edwardian villas
under Slieve Martin – its curled up forests
reflecting sleepily in the Lough.
The winter day sinks into a crescent
of light, between North and South.

Upstream of Warrenpoint
a black line leaves the map,
disintegrates to specks
drifting apart, dissolving,
sweeping down the narrows
to the sea.

Cold fills the North.
The clouds move briskly.
Carlingford Mountain
shrinks into itself
like a child expecting
a blow.

Something emerges from the grass behind it,
whimpering, shivering; wet fur clings in streaks
parting to show the skin, shifting and changing
shape, a pitiful trail scraped by the wind
moving across the hillside, innocent, lethal;
the scapegoat stumbles off into the dusk.

Leavings

They gather in the street, their faces blanched
by TV lights, their hair streaked by the rain.

      I turn over the driftwood on the beach
      and find that one of the black shapes is a bird.

After the silent vigil they leave flowers
outside the bookie's, heaped on the pavement and steps.

      The bird struggles and tries to launch itself
      into the boiling surf, and falls back.

The steel shutter stays closed. There are children's poems
cellotaped to it, with the names of the dead.

      The tide goes out. The bird is left gasping,
      wings trailing at odd angles, drowning on sand.

The wind dislodges the carefully placed bouquets.
Rain seeps into the centre of each flower.

      Perhaps the wings are broken. They twitch and go still.
      The eyes' angry brightness begins to fade.

Carnations. Roses. Chrysanthemums. Steady rain
crushes the petals, turning their gloss to pulp.

Crows will pick out the eyes. The next high tide
will nudge the heap of feathers and set it afloat.

When the bin men come, drowned petals and frayed stems
will go with the ash to be landfill in Belfast Lough.

Tremors

The bomb exploded a mile and a half away
 – our house twitched slightly, dust fell from the ceiling.
Two men were murdered at the Cleansing Depot
 – for days our street was full of bins not emptied.

Always the epicentre is somewhere else
 – only the tremors reach us, gruesome, banal,
like the Red Hand of Ulster at Mount Stewart
Gardens, set with tired geraniums.

It's the hand I think of. The woman who lost two fingers
in the blast. She appeared in the paper, nameless,
ousted next day by more casualties, more dead.
Patched up by plastic surgery, Valium,

and prayer, will she pull her life together,
picking her way through a web of absences?
I start to notice people's hands, as if
hers with its awkward gap – scars not yet healed –

is waiting for me. In the newsagent's
she's the one who can't untie a knot
to lay out a stack of papers. She hands me change
cautiously; a coin rolls to the floor.

At lunchtime in the pub, she balances
a glass, but can't quite manage knife and fork.
At the school gates she takes her children's hands,
flinching as they touch where it's still sore.

In church she kneels beside me at the rail,
holding her cupped hands to receive the wafer,
the fingers of one hand lightly cradling the other,
tilted slightly; trembling with the strain.

Everything she touches bears the print
of grief, bewilderment, courage. My own hands
ache in this bitter wind. My fingers itch
and then turn numb, as if they were already gone.

Till Only the Eyes Are Left

The muttering kept me awake
three nights, then resolved itself
into a black wind –
catching the road off balance
slamming it into walls
freezing it scalding it lifting
the skin from the roof of its mouth.

Then it went quiet. I stood
at our back door. The wind
came whining into our yard
– a stray dog begging scraps.

Get out. I won't feed you.
I've seen you snarling, worrying
clusters of dead newsprint
tossing them up till they catch
in the apple tree, its branches
like barbed wire skewering
sentences, faces.

I watch the pictures split
again and again, till nothing
is left but the eyes of the dead
glowing like tiny lights

in the wet November dusk.
I turn my back on the tree
half hoping half afraid
the black wind might blow them
away, but their reflections
in the glass pane of the door
keep burning steadily.

I will draw the curtains across
every window in the house
and every night for a month
the faintest of noises will wake me:
the wings of moths rustling,
or the doors of an Advent calendar
closing one by one.

The Air Raid Shelter

At the edge of her childhood garden
it squatted, smooth-backed, ominous,
a hollow hill enclosing
claustrophobia, dampness,
woodlice, the smell of fear.

After the War she watched
her father with spade and pickaxe
cave in the roof, bring barrows
of top-soil to bury the darkness,
crushing its concrete ribs
under a mound of flowers,
Grape Hyacinth, Spring Snowflake,
Lavender, Forest Flame, bright
unwinking Forget-me-nots, strange
crab-shell-coloured Anemones.

Her parents are dead now. The bombings
have started again. In her dreams
she hears whimpering, sees petals
shivering, heaving, the mound
cracks open, the tiny hands
of abandoned children, blackened
by long years underground,
struggle out, unrecognisable.

She loses them and finds
drifts of dark, like soot,
filling her house. She hurries
to sweep them back under the roots,
closing the earth down tightly,
and wakes to hear the siren
from the Ormeau Bakery, signalling
the end of the night shift.

We come as refugees
to her house in the long light evenings,
nervous, our fingers clenched
round coffee cups. She sees
the choking dark that once
surrounded us, now crushed
deep inside us, tapping,
restless, like a cancer,
and will fight it if she can,
though her weapons are only flowers
interlacing, blending
frail colours to draw the light
into the earth, for winter.

The Wrong Colour

A litter of stones harassing our feet
as we labour up to the viewing point –
rocks turning slippery, tilting,
screes opening, dragging us backwards.

So it seems entirely logical
when you start to describe the recently
approved plan: *Get rid of the rocks.*
Useless things messing up the landscape

and always the wrong colour – not
the cold clear grey the tourists expect
but a sulky brown, as if they've festered
for years under stagnant water and mud.

I remember days in the high mountains;
ferns and stonecrop in crevices,
thyme and saxifrage spilling over
outcrops the colour of winter dusk.

But here it is never dusk. The light
is always the same. Nothing can grow
on these odd-coloured barren lumps.
My throat is choked, I can't speak

to warn you: if you clear the slopes,
they'll fold in on themselves like soft
flesh without bones, collapsing, sinking,
treacherous as scum on a bog

until the last rock drags the sky
down to clench and knot around it
so that the rain comes. Then all colours
will be the same, and blotted out.

Rosguill

Year after year I return to this windblown country
of perfect miniatures: the cottage crouching
in the lee of a hill, its windows blurred with salt,
its hearth overgrown by forests of jackdaws' leavings
from a chimney-nest: slivers of turf, sheep's wool,
cracked fuschia twigs. Outside, the wheatears
flick from stone to stone of the ruined wall,
the cock reflecting all the shoreline colours:
grey for the water; white – the rake of foam
along the high tide line of black seaweed;
pale tawny gold – the flawless crescent of beach
basking on itself, smooth as new skin.

But not this year. This year the rocks have come –
as if they had been scattered there – or grown
raggedly out of the sand, stubbly black
things gulping for air. I have to nerve
myself to walk straight past and not look back
to see if they're following. I think of night
camouflaging them as they rattle together
like some starved animal's skeleton, growing new fur,
lumbering into the water to be swept
out past the headland, into infinity.

Still every morning finds them on the shore
in their familiar shape, glazed with blown spray,
knowing nothing can shift them, not even the wind
that scours with sand the whole peninsula,
burying villages down the centuries,
nudging the dunes and lifting them to lay bare
earth's old tired bones.

Beltany Stone Circle

The road is a late arrival
among these wise green hillsides.
We climb past headless signposts,
ambiguous, like the white
mist, or smoke, that rises
from roofs, or ridges. Stones
watch from the hilltop, freeze
at our approach, pretending
decrepitude, decay.

They are ears pricked to hear any rumblings
across the hazy miles from Grianan, or the Border.
They are waves petrified, straining outwards,
leaning with the rain towards distant seas.
They are teeth wrenched out of ancient jaws,
planted in new earth to defend a tribe
against enemies, against age, against time itself.
They are shadows raised in stone, for where there are
shadows
there must be light; they have brought down the sun
to seethe in hearths and cooking pots, and keep back
winter.

Their meaning is lost like the bones
and skins and hair that have nourished
this quiet wind-green place.

Annaghmakerrig to Loughareema

A shifty sort of place – unblessed
by science, milk's straight from the cow,
cats muster on all sides, the steps
double themselves in the dark, light-switches
vanish. The lake is out there sulking,
moonless, deep enough to drown in.

This is where your water comes from.
Turn the glass, the silt swirls slowly
and sinks, a blend of sand and what falls
in it – heron feathers, fish scales,
dust from cattle hooves, the crinkled
crisped-up thrown-off last reminders
of beech leaves, shadows of hills that might be
concealed behind these trees. All summer
flies got stuck on the surface, thrashing
about with delicate wings, despairingly
bumping against your lips as you failed
to drink it. Left the glass to steam
on a hot windowsill. Awoke to find
yourself transported all the way
from Annaghmakerrig to Loughareema,
the Vanishing Lake – the flies embedded
in sediment rapidly drying, yourself
crawling about among flakes of mud,
the bed too deep, you grown too tiny
ever to get up the sides of the glass.

Not Having Danced All Night

She stepped up to the mike. They dimmed the lights
so only her face stood out in ridges and hollows
 – landscape, not skin: a gleaming sandbank lapped
by midnight sea. They even picked up
the waves, uncannily real, on the synthesizer,
and as she sang I heard the sigh and hiss
of water rushing in to fill the room
with starfish, mermaids' purses, arrow-worms,
sea-wrack swishing against my hands as I flattened
them over my ears to block out the noise of the surf
but it battered on in my head, insistent, maddening –

They pulled out all the leads. The rhythm faded,
the lights came up, the room was high and dry
and cold as dawn. The singer had already left
and out in the street I could hear the cheerful clatter
of the boys loading the van up with dismembered
equipment, shiny, sleek, no sign of rust,
no ripple marks etched on the well-worn roadway.

Everything looked like itself and was perfectly quiet.
I shook my head. No waves. No buzzing. Nothing
that couldn't be reduced to its components,
stowed in a sealed compartment in my brain.

But my feet were aching from not having danced all night,
I caught them out looking for sand in the gutters
and paddling the grass as gulls do, trying to lure
worms up from the depths with a promise of rain.

Translating

As far as Chekhov's concerned
– my Russian teacher said –
the sky is either blue
or it isn't.
          No poetry.
Sentences that stand
like clipped trees on the skyline,
casting well-defined shadows.
Workmanlike, easily
translated.
          Barely touched on
here, is the whole dimension
you might call feminine –
the shifting interplay
of colours, at the edges
of shadows, a mood passing,
grey merging with green,
a sentence qualified
by a web of roots, of tiny
branches all mixed up
with clouds that won't stay still
for a moment, to be translated
into words, let alone English.

This Room is Closing Now

Here, under glass, a flourish of stems and leaves
transfixed by a typed label: English or Irish,
Fifteenth or Sixteenth Century. Every stitch
as bright as if it had ripened just this morning

under her careful needle. We gaze and gaze
as if her whole life's preserved behind glass: perhaps
it was; English or Irish, sitting for years
with her back to the fire, her face to the flickering window

whose small crabbed panes would hide and reveal the shapes
of what might be horses grazing, or the wind
caught in the blackthorn bushes, or crouched figures
in the dusk, surrounding the tower. But at her feet

the wolfhounds slept on undisturbed, their coats
tangled with the silks that spilled from her clawed
arthritic hands, as she rested between births,
her crippled body too stiff for the narrow stairs,

she worked while daylight lasted, and when the sun
touched the marsh to gold, she thought of fire
in the thatch, wood smouldering, flaring up, the glass
splintering and slivers of it seeming

to lodge in her gut where the pain twisted and deepened
and the bleeding would not stop. Day after day
it was draining out of her, soft and dark and cold
as the damp that seeped through the tapestry from the stones,

and still her needle laboured to create
herself pacing among the clipped yew hedges,
her hand on the collar of some heraldic beast
in a garden of herbs, St John's wort, rosemary,

camomile, comfrey, simples for every ill,
fruits without blemish, flowers of burnished gold
and the baby curled inside her, static and proud
as the shining curves of the phoenix in the tree –

or so it seems to us, as the attendant
covers the glass – 'This room is closing now' –
and we make for the exit, a wet October night,
the swish of tyres, the street lights going on.

Female Nude

From where she lies, she can just see the edge of the window.
She's watched the swifts lacing the sky with black threads,
travelling South and returning so many times
in the time it has taken him to re-arrange
her body: compliant limbs spreading and rippling
in a square of light that gives her flesh the sheen
of an over-ripe peach, gold, with a bloom of dust.
He's been gone ages now. The smell of turps,
oil paint, the smoke from his pipe, disperse in the draught
from the rattling window. She lumbers to her feet,
stiff, after lying still for centuries.

The thing won't close.
Down in the street,
running, hustling,
a crowd of women –
thin and tense.
Greyhounds. Gazelles.
We can do it
stamped on their T shirts.
Working, sweating,
honing their flesh,
their gleaming limbs
jerk as if pulled
by invisible strings.

The ad man's dream –
the puppet master?
She strains at the window.

Still it won't close and their high-pitched voices reach her
 – bossy, nervy creatures in love with movement.
She cannot join them, all she can do is imagine
him with his tired frown, sighing, throwing a cloth
over the easel, knotting the puppet strings
to the bars of the window, but loosely, so that they slip
little by little into the street below.

A Brown Moth

She sees a window at midnight
suddenly break into light,
a flourish of golden petals
to open and ripple and scatter
their sweet dust over her wings
as she crawls towards the centre –

there is no centre. The limit
of the glass gives way to cold
air, echoing, empty,
a confusion of lights. She blunders
from one to the next, off balance,
spinning desperately,

a moon lurching out of orbit,
lost among so many planets,
her brown wings thrashing, changing
their shape like shreds of colour
caught in a kaleidoscope,
disintegrating, flickering,

to settle back at last
into the old, known curves,
folded, self-effacing
as cobwebs under leaves,
crevices of bark,
patterns of sunlight on dust.

Pavement

The paving stones become huge fields, divided
by ditches, as the child teeters across
in her mother's high-heeled shoes. Her tiny feet
slop from side to side; one shoe capsizes
and pulls her down outside the greengrocer's,
trays of fruit cascading round her, oranges
scuttling into the gutter, each a world
rolling out of her reach, dimpled and ridged
with puddles, hillsides, clumps of yellow grass.

Inside her head, her mother scolds. Slowly
the bright globes diminish to background. The child
hobbles painfully homewards in the shoes:
a half-tame pony, tethered to a threadbare
shrinking verge, by these beautiful useless symbols.

A Different Father

Friday. Kept in again,
avoiding my eye and the page,
he's written 10th March, his name,
and made thirty holes in the floor
with a pair of compasses.

The others are romping home:
his sleek brothers and sisters,
fast workers, tossing
their schoolbags over the hedge.
He stays in his corner,

a twilight cave where he crouches
shaggy and bloated, among
chewed pencils, dismembered bones,
ignores passing dinosaurs.
It's not that he's stupid,

his mother asserts. *He just
won't work. It all runs off him
like water off a duck's back.
He had a different father
from the others, you know.*

Yes. The others are high
fliers, and he is grounded
like a moulting drake in a pond.
We throw crusts of information.
He picks them up, drops them.

Head mostly under his wing.
Our feeble scoldings muffled
by raggedy feathers. Warm
close-to-the-body darkness.
He gazes into it,

blinks, tries to make out
a fading image: a big
man with a slow smile
hoisting his tiny son
on to solid shoulders.

Next of Kin

I decide to fancy David. There's no harm
in it: he's gay, our resident novelist,
I can spend all night in his pocket keeping warm,
distracting myself with a feeling that won't last

longer than this writing weekend, where
I feel like a limpet prised from a rock, afloat
in a sea of concepts English has no words for –
it's not quite *psyche*, *soul* or even *heart* –

'They're all wrong,' someone says. 'There isn't a word
for deep inside you, where you feel things most.'
I sit self-consciously at the edge of the crowd,
missing my husband, suddenly tired and lost

in a cold tight layer of air, feeling the lack
not deep inside, but in the shivers that stray
across face, shoulders, hands, the back of my neck,
all those places where no-one's touching me.

Later, David shuts himself away
with a pile of our scripts to read, and on his door
Do Not Disturb Except In Emergency.
I sit and write and sit and tilt my chair,

longing for someone to come and disturb me with
"Your husband rang", an understanding smile,
a conspiratorial grin that says we both
know how it feels. Like that time in hospital

after visiting hours, trying to have a laugh
with any nurse who'd pause and make a few
feeble cracks about "my other half."
The phone, that was silent then, is ringing now:

I grab it. Gasp. A man's voice. But not his.
'Can I speak to David? It's his home.'
I start to say, "He's not…" and stop. Your voice
has a loneliness deeper than any I've known.

'I need to speak to David.' Who are you?
Not the familiar mortgage and joint account
other half, the one with the same name, who
they'd send for if doctors and nurses were fussing round

David, in hospital, wiring him up to machines.
You'll never be next of kin. No. You're
just next to his heart, or soul, whatever that means,
whatever it is that English has no words for.

Chevaux-de-Frise

Some people's defences are an art form.
Yours are more physical. You've backed away
till your retreat is cut off by the sea
and what you can't ignore becomes a storm

battering this promontory. It provides
a chance for us to discuss the weather, as if
it's Out There, not inside us. Then a brief
lull in the storm, at dusk, the wind subsides

and leaves me sitting on the landward side
in front of all these stones forbiddingly
stuck in the ground like stakes for the cavalry
to stumble over. But they've had their last ride

and my pain is lessened because I've found the name
for the spiky stones in some book: *chevaux-de-frise*.
I stare at the sea and wonder how long this truce
will have to last, before the urge to blame

is forgotten, and you lurch to your feet, thirst-crazed,
concentrating hard as you thread your way,
cursing, bruising your shins, breathing heavily,
out through the stubborn remnants of this maze.

The Scratch

Flaunting their richness of age, their almost-perfection,
the Persian rugs glow with their stained-glass colours:
amber, russet, crimson, faultless crescents,
arches, flights of steps, all delicately
balanced, one deliberate black knot spoiling
the symmetry. 'Allah alone is perfect.'

Even the early settlers in New England
gathered their patient triangles of patchwork
into a flourish of little horses ramping
across striped winter fields – but sewed wrong colours
into the final row, fearing to challenge
the powerful, obtuse God they imagined.

You have no such Gods.
No need to fear achieving
perfection. What you give
me is spoiled already;
a tiny marble box,
its careful lustrous curves
intricately patterned –
a jagged white mark
scored across their smoothness.
I lick my finger and rub;
the scratch dissolves like salt.

The wetness dries; the scratch
re-makes itself, rough edged,
permanent as a scar.

If I gaze long enough, I can see the whole pattern move –
crawling with moss and sand and rust and silver
melting into each other, under the thin
streak that is like the single slash of white
where bark has been torn from a tree trunk, opening
up the whole forest, drawing the eye on into
deep shadows where the movement of every leaf
creates new colours I've never seen before.

A Ring with a Black Stone

A hairsbreadth round my finger, a constriction
slight as an indrawn breath – until it tightens
as stitches do in a wound, making my flesh swell
and try to break the fine thread or absorb it,
dissolve it in my blood; but it will never
allow itself to be devoured by me –
the thread is you, stubbornly separate,
facing me with your differentness, your challenge.

The stone set in this ring stares back at you,
uncompromisingly; no diamonds
to sparkle with their easy open-all-hours
smile, their breathless promise of eternal
availability. Instead, a black stone
squats like a sea anemone on dry rocks,
bedraggled, sulky, drained of all its colour,
its petals clenched in tight against you, waiting

in its dull weekday silence, for the moment
when a wave rises and spills its dazzle across
the petals, they unfold, the light slants into
each facet of the black stone and discovers
a sapphire: mist uncurling, iridescent,
a gasp of blue flicked from a magpie's feathers
as it opens a curious eye and reaches to gather
all the bright fragments and threads of colour you bring.

After the Marriage

1

It sparkled like a white Venetian palace,
trefoils and curves, a wedding cake of stone
iced with new rainbows. They were never selfish,
they wouldn't keep it for themselves alone;
they opened it to students and to tourists
and lost ones looking for a place to stay.
Wave-nibbled stilts raised it above the water
that smelt of green and August and decay.
Right from the first it needed scaffolding,
it couldn't stand the weight they made it bear,
and after years of worry and expense
they found the fragile stones beyond repair,
and watched the gleam of their brave fantasy
crumble, and touch the greyness of the sea.

2

His single bed creaks though there's no-one in it.
The fan hums all night in his hotel room.
He shakes his fingers, coughs, to clear the sticky
membranes clinging round him like a womb.
This is what's left of all they'd built: the slimy
trails in the water, stumps of rotting wood.
She dips her oars in grey and green, the subtle

colours of sea he never understood
and pulls away. Her boat spins in the current,
always dragged back. He feels her sea-sickness
from far away, churning in his own stomach
as he moves inland, sees her drowning face
in every paving stone. The streets are bare.
The light becomes the colour of her hair.

3

That was when you started to look for me.
Thought I'd be cold, you said. You still couldn't grasp
my need to be always out-of-season, moving
in random circles, sifting through the past
at the expense of the future, feeling the chill
currents sweep me past each landing stage.
That was my freedom; yours was walking slowly
past the lighted windows of each cage
calling them *houses*, trying to get inside.
But space grew wider round you however close
to the warmth you tried to get. And space clenched in
round me, confined me, thickened to enclose
my solitude, my fear that I would choke
on fear – my own, or yours. The pattern broke

4

when I caught you by the arm, crying *Leave me alone.*
We found ourselves in an empty echoing square
with a winter feel to it, all the cafés shuttered,
a litter of closed-up parasols and chairs
lapping the edges of buildings like a tide –
but you had given up on buildings, I
had given up on water. Pigeons' wings
fretted, scribbled, smudged the darkening sky,
writhing and settling like snowflakes, grey on grey.
White is a lie, you said. *A trick of the light.*
Can't last. And *Neither can movement*, I said.
My fingers froze in yours. Only the slight
nudge of your pulse disturbed me, offering
the rhythm of the tide beneath your skin.

Synchronizing

Two single sleeping bags:
husks of our former lives,
smelling of heather, grass
curled in unvisited corners –

even here in the dark they are fading,
shrivelling, wearing away
to nothing, ready to split
as the skin of a chrysalis

bursts, and a clutched dampness
of daylight heaves itself out
and opens into wings
that shimmer and pulse with light.

This is where we sleep
now, in a fan of soft
colours that ripple and spread
around us all night long

and even in sleep we adjust
our bodies to perfect balance,
synchronizing our breath
so that neither wing will drag

on the other, send the whole
thing tilting and careering
lopsidedly towards
winter, or wherever

we left those narrow husks
of our old, clenched-in selves
each lying alone, staring
into the creaking dark.

Losing Count

I watch the miles unravel,
strung with beads of brightness
flicking through the sea mist:

seventeen – a sail,
a leaping dolphin's back,
somewhere close inshore,

twenty – gannets diving,
fulmars chuckling on ledges
along the basalt cliffs,

forty – a waterfall
plunging through the bracken
sheer into the sea,

fifty – crumpled rock
scattered round our wheels,
and the road ebbing inland

to tally with names from the guide book:
The Blue Glen, Field of the Bramble,
Hill of the Two Winds.

Somewhere we must have crossed
the Ford of the Stranger. Numbers
are sliding off the dashboard

losing their digital clarity,
furring up like the bodies
of moths smashed on the windscreen.

It's time to leave the car
and go on foot. The sky
heaving itself from the fog

is unexpected, luminous,
glazed with afterblue,
the mountains ripening,

the sun at our backs dissolving
distances, drawing horizons
of tawny and gold towards us.

The Irish Dancers

Discarded jumpers, kicked-off shoes,
empty glasses: the evening's silt
is all pushed back to line the walls
as a troupe of girls in embroidered dresses
sidle into the space and stand
whispering shuffling pawing the ground
staring at their feet until
the music starts.
                    It takes them over –
zigzags circles spirals ripples
till the harps and shamrocks they're all got up in
fuse into pure curve, pure colour,
their flushed intent faces bobbing
on a wave of turquoise, scarlet, gold,
they're swimming downstream, shooting the rapids
– then it always happens:
                    the tape runs out
too soon, and leaves them tapping
their last steps into the silence,
or their steps run out, they're left blushing
in a clatter of un-danced-to notes.
We clap. They smile, subside, relax.

You know what it puts me in mind of? The way
you and I slide into bed,
sweep away the quilts, the daylight,

catch the beat until it lifts
into something else –

                    the pulse of a high
tide making towards the shore
with us in its undertow, eyes closed,
losing track of who's calling the tune
and who's dancing –

                    and then one
pair of eyes opens, the other stays
oblivious, till the dance is over.
We hold each other, tolerant,
replete – neither insists that next time
the endings must tally, or that we need
a better stage than this clearing among
encroaching quilts, newspapers, clothes,
or a better audience than each other.

Woman as Flower

Trapped in the ageing metaphor
of woman as flower, you stand
rooted and blooming doggedly
on, in earth that has hardened
and frozen like the smile
of your outstretched rigid shivering
petals.
       Inside them, nothing.
No ripe fruit swelled in you
to burst and thrust its seeds out
into the hazy uncertain
autumn. Only brown stains
spreading like the shadows
under eyelids, veined
with a little dust as fragrant
as spice, spilt and forgotten
in a closed cupboard.
             But you
stay fiercely open. Your hunger
is deeper than emptiness,
it pulls and sucks at the air
till wingbeats, woodsmoke, sparks,
the fur of rain, the curve
of light, the vast clear sky,
flow down towards your centre
and settle themselves in your hollow.

August Letter

A Donegal beach
too small to have a name
is sliding into dusk
and as I move away

my shoulders twitch; something
flicks at the corner of my eye,
it leaps behind me, white
with its own light –

on the wind-sheared sand,
stillborn, a river,
slight as a footprint,
curved as marram grass,

it sneaks towards the sea
like an old superstition:
look, a long white thread,
that means you'll get a letter.

 – Send it when I'm hurrying
through heavy streets, breathing
fast, fumes and dust,
loaded with strident voices;

show me the vein of a leaf
uncurling, pleading,
almost dry, the ghost
of water following me.

Childless

Slinky, screeching, dark, they skite about
like swifts in next door's garden, following
their flightpaths through an airspace that can turn
solid for them to slide on, hang from, swing –

or wanting the sound of the waves, they redesign
their strip of grass and bushes as an island,
they prance into the spray and scurry back,
bedraggled, damp, to catch hold of her hand.

'Mummy, he says I'm ugly.' 'He says I'm a girn.'
'Well then don't play with him. There's other fish
in the sea.' The kitchen window is a lighthouse,
from far out in their boat they see it flash

as they tack unsteadily across the garden,
then the real rain starts. I hear her call them in.
I watch the walls of their house bulge and turn liquid
with laughter, till the rooms rock up and down.

Our house is childless. Rooms have never stretched
nor walls dissolved. These mornings we sleep long
in a bed engulfed by sand. Each month we carve
fantastic shapes and wait for the tide's tongue

to snake up the moat and lick the sides till they crumble
under the sea's huge swirling swishing run,
hemming us in and dragging us out and crowding us
to the edges of our lives. But it never comes.

Because of the sea's absence we hear the wind
louder and louder all night, becoming the voice
of absence itself, commenting on the dull
parade of space after space after space after space.

Ghost Train

(1)

After the first X-ray,
the doctor demonstrates:
These (crooking his arms)
are your fallopian tubes
and these (flexing his fingers)
are fimbria. This is where
(if your tubes were open)
the dye would come oozing out…

I dream of the hospital:
the darkened ward contracts,
becomes my womb, with me
scrabbling at walls to find
openings, passages – dragged
into a childhood memory
– the ghost train slithering
through tunnels dimly lit
by the faint luminous seepage
of blue dye – feathery
fingers brushing my face –
gone before I can catch them –
scarlet letters flashing
on doors, forming words
in an unknown alphabet –
just as it starts to make sense,

a man in a white coat
flicks a switch. The words
shiver, distort, dissolve
and every door I come to
is smooth and black and closed.

(2)

Even the anaesthetist
can't find my veins. They shrink
at the first touch of the needle,
retreating like a snail's
antennae, into a shell
of deceptively docile flesh
and the sensible voice in my head
– *For your own good* – fails
to draw them out again.

When I finally go under,
I dream I'm giving birth:
Push, they say, and I push.
Out come streams of sparks
hissing and spitting, then
scarlet tongues of flame
sliding from sheet to floor
– these are my veins, crackling
coiling seething jumping,
intent on their spectral dance
of blood and flickering light.

Out of Our Reach

A salmon slides out of me. It looks half dead.
It's another dream about giving birth. I catch
the creature and cradle it in an embroidered sheath
as if it's a sword in a scabbard – only the eyes
are like eyes in Renaissance paintings that seem to follow
your movements round the room. It suddenly leaps
in a silver arc to the floor, twists, turns, flaps, writhes
at my feet. When I stoop to pick it up, it's covered
in dust, and I can't make out if it's still breathing.

I wake up. Feel the darkness ebb away
from my head. Sunlight replaces it, benign,
motionless, reassuring. I sit down
among the houseplants. Stroke the cat. Drink coffee.
Then the cat goes haywire, leaping, hurling
herself in the air, grasping at something always
just above the blurred flash of her paws:
a butterfly sun, making tiny spangles of light
flick from the tilting surface of my cup
wildly up and down walls, across the ceiling.

I finish the coffee. The cat keeps stretching, baffled,
gazing up in delicious uncertainty.
It's me who carries what certainties there are:
that fish can't breathe in air, that I can't breathe
in water, that the sun will always find
some scrap of liquid, metal, glass, to send
its brief reflections dancing out of our reach.

Scars

A stone falls into a pool, sudden and sharp
– it might be the careless flick of a salmon leaping –
the water closes cleanly, leaves no trace.

I try to curl up in this dream, as circles
diminish, stroked to smoothness by the light,
but my mind stumbles over a puckered surface

where ripples harden into ridges and furrows
of salt that fret and grind against the rocks
till my body is sand, with all the uneasiness

of sea gnawing the coastline, struggling to tear
the dunes apart – but thin tough stems secure them
with loops of grass-stitch, set with small bright flowers

– sea milkwort, creeping cinquefoil, silverweed –
holding their ground as the pale grains shift and settle
to form the scars and contours of the future.

Reclaimed Land

The end of the line. Rust
flakes from the tangled tracks
skewed across a barren
spit of scrawny shingle.

I search for plovers' eggs,
freckled among the stones;
find only the wind, scraping
the endless greyness, battering

abandoned goods trucks.
Shelter. The rotting planks
disclose a tentative circle
of green, edging outwards:

gorse, bramble, some tiny
tenacious saltproof plant
with feathery leaves, asserting
the survival of small things.

Warmed by a moment's sunshine,
a white butterfly
pauses among the nettles.
A twist of silver paper

and the ring-pull from a can
I take as evidence
that other survivors passed
this way, and will again.

Madonna of the Spaces

Botticelli might have painted
her thoughtful tawny eyes
and capable sunburnt hands
in her lap, cradling nothing.

after several botched attempts,
the baby's chubby limbs
and petulant sleepy face
have finally been erased,

leaving an aureole –
faint gold flecks of dust
fading to a halo-shaped
dent in the canvas

through which the weather pushes
its tangled, damp threads –
a promise of water flicking
in and out of willows,

playing with the reflections
of women who kneel at the edge
and wash clothes and gossip
into the blue distance.

This is what she sees –
figures trudging up crazy
goat paths to the walled
city. Market day.

Shoulders braced to the weight
of baskets. Through the mesh
something shining – fish,
olives, damsons, grapes?

She stretches, flexing her wrists,
wanting to follow but held
back by the suspicion
that they've been trying to harvest

the sparkle of light from the river,
stuffing it into their panniers
and it pouring out as fast,
tumbling down the rocks,

leaving a silver trail,
till every basket holds
simply the shape of itself
sculptured in emptiness.

The Aphrodite Stone

The stone is what I've salvaged
from winter-bruised Akamas, the limestone cliffs
that curl into caves and grottoes, crumble
into a wave-locked Burren where thistle and thorn
nuzzle apart the vertebrae of rock
and the tide is all the music
of pebbles grinding churning abrading hammering
holes in each other.

The stone is a sculpture
by Henry Moore, with a gap hollowed out
where the heart and guts should be.

The stone is a woman
crouched on the edge of the bed. She cradles
her breasts that still hang heavy, blindly seeking
tiny mouths to suck, refusing to be
comforted, refusing to know
that the child was never a child but a clot of blood
ebbing out of her
leaving a cavity
for the wind to whistle through.

The stone is a souvenir
from Aphrodite's birthplace from the rock
where she perched like a mermaid posing for the tourists
till her honey-coloured flesh faded to grey
weathered fractured fissured pock-marked pocketed
into holes and then worn smooth
by the undertow,
abandoned
above high water mark.

The stone says: Hold me
in the hollow of your hand.